EMBRACE THE STRUGGLE

ARTI KUMAWAT

We all live in the same planet, yet some people hide their faces or either moving away from their struggles and some is positive and confident to overcome their obstacles. Anyone who faces with a struggle in their life is in a continual battle and only the one who stands firmly through all the barriers will be victorious in the end. I think that even with all the power and understanding we have, if one gives up their life simply because of their struggle, then that person also lacks hope and courage to fight against their barrier and he or she definitely fails. Knowledge to me in high school is not limited in the eight specific courses we take but nevertheless the significance of wisdom and striving to expand our global perspectives also becomes another step in shattering the brick wall in my life. However, we must know when to retreat when necessary because if we wish to advance and triumph over our struggle as rapidly as possible, this may result in the lost of your battle. I truly believe this simply because a struggle is an obstacle in our life, we should enjoy the challenges that we're face with rather than quickly overcoming your struggle. Now I begin to understand how to manipulate my struggles correctly so therefore it will become a solution in the future. My struggle symbolizes a compass, it correctly shows the path of my life and it serves as a force of motivation that pushes me to prevail over my struggle. So , let's talk about simple important things about Struggle .

Contents

Contents

Contents

Contents

Contents

Foreword

<u>Life Is Full Of Struggles</u>

There are days that truly bring us down
We sit and mop and constantly frown
The issues we face right now are overwhelming
We feel like jumping up and running.

But running away doesn't take away the pain
Running away only makes us feel more drained
Find that glimmer of hope
Focus on that it will help you cope.

Rather than sitting and feeling sad
Take action don't get mad
Find a way to take one step
Towards the thing called happiness.

You see life is full of struggles and hurt
There are times we all feel like dirt.
But don't stay down, get up and find
A change of thought of the positive kind.

It may not be easy to get back on your feet
But moving forward, step by step can be sweet.
One foot in front of the other can be
Better than sitting and pouting you will see.

So even though the struggles you face
Don't give in and lose the pace.
Let your determination show
Even if your progress is slow.

The day will come when good times roll
One step at a time you will reach your goal
So when you see a challenge coming your way
Remember this too shall pass, you shall say!

"Struggle" and "Success" , both the words are similar , if we have to know about them . Struggle is not only make trouble in our life but it teaches us that how can we hold any kind of situation that is depend on yourself and that's the main work of struggle to make you strong and your future bright. Sometimes we take it wrong and not understand it clearly because we should not hear good criteria for our life. Success is come in our life but only after struggle so , you cannot ignore the fact that struggle is most important for achieving our goal .Writer struggled and still struggling because she start her work and in between she faces a lot of difficulties during working but she have a confidence on her so she decided to never fail in her life . Depend upon our situation that how we faced it but that's not mean , we're failed, always be confident and doing different things in your life for your future and decide how can you treat yourself regarding your future and Success. But before this we have to understand ,"What is Life?"-

What is Life ?

First of all, Life refers to an aspect of existence. This aspect processes acts, evaluates, and evolves through growth. Life is what distinguishes humans from inorganic matter. Some individuals certainly enjoy free will in Life. Others like slaves and prisoners don't have that privilege. However, Life isn't just about living independently in society. It is certainly much more than that. Hence, quality of Life carries huge importance. Above all, the ultimate purpose should be to live a meaningful life. A meaningful life is one which allows us to connect with our deeper self.

One important aspect of Life is that it keeps going forward. This means nothing is permanent. Hence, there should be a reason to stay in dejection. A happy occasion will come to pass, just like a sad one. Above all, one must be optimistic no matter how bad things get. This is because nothing will stay forever. Every situation, occasion, and event shall pass. This is certainly a beauty of Life.

Many people become very sad because of failures. However, these people certainly fail to see the bright side. The bright side is that there is a reason for every failure. Therefore, every failure teaches us a valuable lesson. This means every failure builds experience. This experience is what improves the skills and efficiency of humans.

Probably a huge number of individuals complain that Life is a pain. Many people believe that the word pain is a synonym for Life. However, it is pain that makes us stronger. Pain is certainly an excellent way of increasing mental resilience. Above all, pain enriches the mind.

The uncertainty of death is what makes life so precious. No one knows the hour of one's death. This probably is the most important reason to live life to the fullest. Staying in depression or being a workaholic is an utter wastage of Life. One must certainly enjoy the beautiful blessings of Life before death overtakes.

Life is beautiful but not always easy, it has problems, too, and the challenge lies in facing them with courage, letting the beauty of life act like a balm, which makes the pain bearable, during trying times, by providing hope

Happiness, sorrow, victory, defeat, day-night are the two sides of the me coin. Similarly life is full of moments of joy, pleasure, success and comfort punctuated by misery, defeat, failures and problems. There is no human being on Earth, strong, powerful, wise or rich, who has not experienced, struggle, suffering or failure.

Life is the precious gift that needs to be spent for the right purpose and goals for valued success and achievements. Life is one word that comes with multiple meanings. Life has different definitions and different people belonging to different field define it differently. There are many perceptive to see life. Life is continuity. It is journey from birth to death. Philosophers and religious people may define it somewhat more differently. Life is basically based on ones thoughts about it. Life is mixture of pains and happiness called ups and downs. These are basis of life. Life is truly a challenge and one has to cope with different problems and circumstances in life. Life is in itself a name of change. Conditions are not same all the time. It is very important to lead a meaningful life.One should be focused on his dreams and must not go astray. Sometimes it is harsh while next second it is joyful. One has rightly said "life is a pendulum between pains and happiness" One has to face all the conditions manfully in his life. We do not remain in same condition all the time. Success is for those who faces these problems manfully.

We all wanted to be successful in life and success is main factor of life. Success demands hard work and passion. We all have our dreams and goals in our life and we want to achieve them. All our life we struggle for success. Hard work is a key to success and takes man to the pinnacle of success. There is no doubt there will be no gain without pain. It is only when toils and sweats it out that success is nourished and sustained. Failures are also part of time. One should not lose hope and learn from failures and mistakes. It is also step toward success if we learn from it. It is important to be optimistic in life. We should always look at the brighter side of life. We should not be depressed at nasty conditions instead accept them manfully. It is important to believe in beauty of dreams for successful life. One should keep working for his sacred dreams. It is important to live a managed life for success. It is also to value time in life as it is important factor for success.

Happy life is not difficult to live if we understand the basic concept of life. Happy life is contented life. One should not blindly run after worldly fame and money.Money is not a purpose for life. It is just need. A basic character of happy life is helping others. It is very important to do something for betterment of humanity. All the great people of past devote their lives for humanity and are now remembered as heroes. It is very important that man should be suppliant.He must not grudge or complain against God. Losses and problems are part of life. It should be dealt open hearted. Happy life is basically balanced life. A person who is at better relationship with family and friends enjoys life better and beautifully.

Life is beautiful but not always easy, it has problems too. Difficulties test our patience, courage, perseverance and true character of a human being. Adversity and hardships make a person strong and ready to face challenges of this world. To sum up, life is beautiful as roses but it has challenges like thorns and has to face and overcome by all. Those who bear great pains and difficulties with patience know the true meaning of life and live their life in true sense. Thus, one should enjoy life but always be ready to cope with problems.

Life is a blessing that creates the difference between the living being and inanimate objects. It gives us the golden opportunity to enjoy the beauty of this earth. We are sent here to fulfill some of our responsibility. Fulfilling all those duties is the main goal of life. According to many writers, life is a stage where we all are performing our roles. So, we should fix a goal or aim in life. A life without an aim is like a ship without a rudder. We have to understand the value of our life. To survive life cheerfully and independently. There are many things to learn and archive from this life.One can enjoy life in one's way. Life is a combination of various moments. happiness and sadness come round in our life. We have to face many obstacles in our way of life. Solving those problems and stepping forward is the lesson of life.

THE
STRUGGLE
MAKES YOU
STRONGER

Life is a journey that starts with our birth. It is very short to waste and we should enjoy it fully. In this short life, we meet many people. Some of them are erased with the flow of time and some stay till death. the regular incidents, special moments, happiness and sadness, achievements and failures. We have to keep moving on and cope up with everything whatever the situation going on. Life is a place of adventure and you have to participate in it. You have to be pessimistic to enjoy a real meaningful life. We live in a family and we like to stay with them. The human being is a social person and we can't live alone. Again, we have to choose a hobby, a passion, and an aim to carry on. If you can adjust to all your routine work you will be happy.

Human life is full of struggle. It's said that life is not a bed of roses. In a short period, we have to deal with varieties of incidents. Sometimes we have to go through a continuous trial in every step. To obtain success we need to keep patience and study. As life is short, we have to practice good virtue in life. A person with strong and bold characteristics is respected by all. So, we should cultivate the ideal virtues like kindness, humanity, honesty, punctuality, and truthfulness. To develop inner peace of mind meditation will help you. Life is unpredictable and it never follows our plan. So we need to learn from everything. A person should not become depressed after failure and mistakes rather he can use the lesson of failure to proceed further towards success.

Life is excellent yet not in every case simple, it has issues, as well, and the test lies in confronting them with mental fortitude, letting the excellence of life behave like an emollient, which makes the torment endurable, during attempting times, by giving expectation

Joy, distress, triumph, rout, day-night are the different sides of the coin. Also, life is loaded with snapshots of bliss, joy, achievement and solace accentuated by hopelessness, rout, disappointments and issues. There is no person on Earth, solid, amazing, savvy or rich, who has not experienced, battle, enduring or disappointed.

Troubles test the mental fortitude, persistence, determination and genuine character of an individual. Affliction and difficulties make an individual solid and prepared to confront the difficulties of existence with poise. Everything comes with a cost in life. It is just when one works and works it out that achievement is supported and maintained.

In this way, life is and ought not to be only a walk in the park; thistles are additionally a piece of it and ought to be acknowledged by us similarly as we acknowledge the delightful side of life.

One significant part of Life is that it continues to go ahead. This amounts to nothing lasting. Subsequently, there ought to be motivated to remain in sadness. A glad event will happen, very much like a pitiful one. Most importantly, one should be hopeful regardless of how terrible things get. This is on the grounds that nothing will remain until the end of time. Each circumstance, event, and occasion will pass. This is surely a stunner of Life.

What does life bring to you?

Life is so natural, yet numerous individuals surge and miss what they need to accomplish throughout everyday life. Try not to surge throughout everyday life. Approach slowly and carefully. Each progression ought to be appropriately arranged prior to being dispatched. Consistent, equilibrium, imprint and shoot.

Every one of the incredible men of today, has for sure tasted the opposite side of life yet they didn't fall down. All things being equal, they were reestablished to reclassify their objectives; they ride on with confidence, having faith in their latent capacity, zeroing in their brain on something, knowing completely well that in each dark cloud there is consistently a silver coating. Numerous individuals become exceptionally tragic on account of disappointments. In any case, these individuals unquestionably neglect to see the splendid side. The brilliant side is that there is a justification for each disappointment. Consequently, every disappointment shows us an important exercise. This implies each disappointment fabricates insight. This experience is the thing that improves the abilities and proficiency of people.

Most likely countless people whine that Life is a torment. Numerous individuals accept that the word torment is equivalent forever. Nonetheless, it is a torment that makes us more grounded. Torment is unquestionably a phenomenal method of expanding mental versatility. Most importantly, torment advances the psyche.

The vulnerability of death is the thing that makes life so valuable. Nobody knows the hour of one's passing. This presumably is the main motivation to make every second count. You are wasting your life if you remain in sorrow or just being a compulsive worker. One should surely appreciate the delightful favors of Life before death surpasses.

Generally significant, hopefulness is a definitive method of improving life. Hopefulness expands work execution, self-assurance, imagination, and abilities. An idealistic individual surely can defeat enormous obstacles.

Contemplation is another helpful method of improving Life quality. Contemplation presumably permits an individual to stay upon his past. This way one can stay away from previous oversights. It additionally gives significant serenity to a person. Moreover, contemplation lessens pressure and strain.

Seeking after a leisure activity is an ideal method to rejuvenate meaning. Without enthusiasm or interest, a person's life would presumably be dull. Following a side interest unquestionably rejuvenates new energy. It gives a new desire to live and encounter Life.

How to face problems in your life ?

1. _Be confident_ :-

Self-confidence refers to the state of mind where a person pushes their boundaries and encourages belief within oneself. Confidence and trust are two interlinking attributes that are mutualistic. The origin of the word 'confidence' is from the Latin word 'fider' meaning trust. Self-confidence makes one independent while having confidence in others helps to build a healthy relationship. Confidence is something that grows with time and experience. It is a strength that requires to be assisted by conviction, passion, and dedication.

Confidence is an amalgamation of trustworthiness, reliability, belief in success, and power to face the consequences. People with greater confidence look healthier and are better suited for any profession, especially when it comes to leadership. Not having enough confidence is not a sign of weakness. True confidence takes time to build and humbleness to retain.Confidence in a person varies with social relationships. An intimidating environment is always in the way of self-confidence, but the friendly and comfortable surrounding is always an aid to confidence. On being studied, it has been reduced that people who have more self-confidence are less likely to conform to others' judgments. With confidence comes the ability to convince people easily and sound affirmative. Children are seen to harbor more' self-confidence because they are often not bothered as much about the consequences of their actions, but teenagers are likely to have a drop in the level of their confidence, often coming from social pressure.

In every field of work, confidence plays an important role. The need to have trust in oneself and the required amount of trust in colleagues is key to better productivity and building a healthy relationship. One is often seen to have high confidence in their strength while being least confident when working with their weaknesses. Even with skill and motivation, lack of confidence is always in the way of fulfilling goals. Lack of self-confidence is a common vulnerability that can be observed in people. At the same time, being overconfident about something also hinders one from attaining their goals.

Confidence helps boost self-esteem and makes it easier for us to be love ourselves and be self-aware. Confidence makes us free from self-doubt and makes us happy with the outcome of our work. With freedom from fear and anxiety, confidence opens the door to have greater strength and capabilities to discover and invent. Confidence builds more peace of mind, improves sleep and health, and guarantees a greater success rate. Higher self-confidence makes it easier to face rejection and constructive criticism. When one has confidence in their hearts, it opens a room for further growth and strength. A sense of security is also felt with confidence.

With being highly beneficial when confidence starts breeding on pride, it takes a toll on a person's mental wellbeing. Overestimating one's worth leads to problematic behaviors and attitudes. Dwelling on overconfidence is more lethal than lacking confidence. There is always room for betterment, but once we become a slave to our ego, it is difficult to go back to being humble about our confidence. Hence, it is important to rightly acknowledge the confidence that we grow in our field of comfort.

Every encounter in life teaches us something, and likewise, with every passing experience, we take home some benefits and knowledge. In this way, confidence in ourselves and others grows. It is alright to be hesitant about trying out new things in life, but when one is willing to attempt something new demonstrates the innate confidence that has always been inside.The state of being clear-headed and confident about something is defined as having confidence in it. Confidence is an attribute that takes time and experience to build and develop. It fluctuates with the various kinds of social circumstances that one has to face.

The fear of failure, not meeting up with one's standards and expectations, builds a lack of confidence. To be confident in oneself and others, one needs 'trust.' Before failure or success is the path that leads to them; journeying through such detours builds the confidence.

Confidence is not only something that builds our personality but also guarantees a better rate of success. Being confident teaches one to be able to handle the emotional outcome of anything one faces. While overconfidence robs us of our humbleness, the lack of confidence makes us fear the simplest things in life. Having the right amount of confidence in our hearts makes life easier, happier, and more fruitful.

Self-confidence is the belief in your own ability when doing anything, by viewing yourself positively and realistically about yourself and your environment. (Densky 2006) In addition, you also need to believe that you have the ability to succeed. (Kent 2007) Self-confidence is also when you feel certain about yourself, your actions, decisions and opinions, and self-reliance. (Hawkins, Swannell & Weston 1998,) Yet, self-confidence is a very useful and powerful tool for everyone to achieve goals and fulfill wishes. Everywhere you go and everything you do, self-confidence is needed for your accomplishment of what you did.

For all these while, many people think that they know what and how self-confidence is, but why some of them could not succeed in what they did. This is because they do not fully understand what self-confidence really is and know the proper and effective ways to improve it. Actually, improving self-confidence is very much depending on one's own self. Moreover, the ways to improve self-confidence are easy as long as you have a strong will to follow and never give up. Hence, self-confidence can be improved through inner of yourself by thinking positively, believing in yourself, setting realistic goals and learning.

Upon understanding what self-confidence is, it is encompasses to know how a self-confident person is. A self-confident person is an optimistic, loving, independent, assertive, eager, self-respect and self-control person, and believe and know well about own abilities. (Mitchell 2007) Physically, a self-confident person looks confident with positive body language and good posture. That are, standing, sitting and walking with straight back, grasping hands in front or back of body, walking with wide steps, firm handshakes, making eye contact and smiling are signs of self-confidence. (2 Know Myself 2007)(Raudsepp 2007) Your viewers will see you confidence and they will have trust in you as you are telling them that "I can do it". When you talk, walk, think behave and feel, self-confidence is shown. (USA Swimming 2004).

In contrast, a lack of self-confidence person is a pessimist, passivity, distrust, perfectionist, sensitive to criticism and failure, inferior, isolated, self-doubt and depressed. (Mitchell 2007) Lack of self-confidence person always put on a sad, worry or confuse look, slump or bend shoulder when sitting and walking, and folding arms, sometimes with crossing legs. (2 Know Myself 2007) These positions labeled you as uncomfortable, unfriendly, annoying and not interesting which caused people around feel the same as you too. Your family members, friends and people around you will unlikely to approach you as you are telling them "Do not come near me", "I can not help you" or "I can not do it". Hence, you should not blame them for ignoring you.

The first and main way to improve your self-confidence is thinking positively. Thinking positively is being happy, healthy with optimism and powerful with hopes. (Lopper 2007) You have to be positive even though you are feeling negative. This is because thinking negatively is very much affecting your self-confident. You may have P's with you when you want to do something, that is, positive because if you always think about negative things, it is sure that you will fail. (USA Swimming 2004) However, this does not mean that you are ignoring the negative events but you accept them, look for the best in the events, and obtain ways to turn them into positive. There, you will see opportunity and hopes to restart again. (Lopper 2007)

Moreover, for an example, you have lost in a competition. No doubt, you were feeling depressed, disappointed, angry, embarrassed, regretful and hopeless, or even worst, want to die. Initially, calm down yourself and recall some happy or past successes in your life included during the competition and success that you desired. When you are recalling, of course, the sad moments of the competition will make you more depressed and emotional. Then, you will keep on asking yourself, "Why am I so stupid?", "I should have done that" or

"Why did I do that?" as these are negative questions that make you feeling negative. Now, you look for way and opportunity by telling yourself, "Yes, I can restart. I shall prepare for the coming next competition. I will try harder this time." Hence, you will feel relief and happy and able to stand up again. Some events such as competition have second round but some events seem like no hope such as lost of family member. However, no matter how, there is always hope and you should forget the past and face the future happily. This is because your family member wants you to continue your life happily.

Firstly, you need to think positively by accepting and loving yourself. If you treat, judge or criticize yourself too cruel, you are lowering down your self-confidence. You should accept, be thankful upon what you have and feel proud of yourself, as there is meaning and value beneath it. Then, you should love yourself by taking care of your health, relaxing, awarding yourself when you have done well and advising yourself if you failed. Hence, you are feeling happy, good and positive with yourself. That is, you have your self-esteem and self-confidence. The most common negative view about oneself is the physical look, that are, not beautiful, not charming, fat body, too short, small eyes or flat nose. You must not compare yourself with others because it is a bad habit where you will forget what is good about you as you comparing you poor criteria with others will put yourself at the weak end. As a result, you will lose your self-confidence. Refer to Dr Sandra Scott, you must not chase after unattainable ideals but feel comfortable with the shape you are. According to Dr. Joe Rubino, accepting and being grateful of what you have, you can eliminate the feeling of incompleteness and dissatisfaction and peace your inner self towards confidence.

Secondly, you also need to think positively about the predicted outcomes. People who are lack of self-confidence are tending to predict the negative outcome before they start doing anything although the reality is not that bad. You must focus on your strengths rather than your weaknesses. For instance, you want to take part in the competition. Before the competition started, because of certain obstacles such as difficulty or feeling threaten by competitors, you predicted that you are not going to win the competition. The reality will not be worst as if you think if you have tried. There are some people claimed that by thinking positively, they even worst, that is, they failed and by thinking negatively can be more successful than thinking positively. These are explainable because they are too focusing on thinking instead of concentrating on what they were doing and they are some people who can use negative thinking to stimulus and challenge themselves. For example using self-talk, "I am scare to lose" or "You have to do it or you will regret". Actually, thinking is your mental preparation before you start to do something. Before you start your 'engine', thinking is the fuel to the 'engine'; hence, you have the power to work for your goal as mental preparation provides you with confidence. As soon as you start, you must concentrate on making your goal alive.

The second way to improve your self-confidence is believing in yourself. That is, you need to think that you have the good in yourself. Hence, you figure out your abilities, strengths, intelligence, achievements or special skills through your interest. (Raudsepp 2007) The lack of ability does not necessary mean that you are lack of self-confidence. (Densky 2006) Therefore, you must believe and discover that you have something more special and powerful than others do, as every human is different. (The National Women's Health Information Center (NWHIC), US 2007) There is no one will always be the best. If you believe that "I can" and not "I can not". If you believe "I am losing", "I can not do this" or "I am out", then you are really out as it is sure that you will not succeed. You must believe that you can be the best of you too.

Another way to improve your self-confidence is setting realistic goals. Realistic goals must be achievable, neither too high nor low. The goals must meet your expectation and demand. Before that, you should understand your ability and create a reasonable standard for yourself. You cannot be good in everything. Too high standards or expectations will gradually weaken one's confidence and have self-doubt. In contrast, too low standards may cause one to be over-confident as he or she will of course feel so easy to reach his or her goals which make he or she think that "I am the best."

Again, another way to improve self-confidence is learning. In order to have self-confidence, you must be willing to learn from experience and new things and keep on learning. Self-confidence does not come immediately as you have to learn. You will not always be the same that is why you need to enhance yourself. Self-confidence is fragile, hence, you learn to maintain it. This can be illustrated by knife which you need to sharpen it sometimes so that you can cut better and easily. For example, you have learned and practice to dance, hence, you can dance gracefully. Then, you stop and dance again after sometimes. You will not dance as graceful as last time but if you willing to learn and practice again, you will dance well again and if you keep on practicing, you even become better and better. When you learn well, you have understood what you do and you do not feel doubt or fear to do it as you have the confidence to do it already. Although you have learn well a skill, you must not stop instead you practice to maintain and develop it. You need to learn forever.

Specifically, you learn from experiences such mistakes, failures, criticisms and successes. Failure always makes ones feel lack of self-confidence. Failure will cause ones to feel. A self-confidence person learns more by making a lot of mistakes and failures. He or she does not scare of failure instead accept the failure and identify the reason of your failing. Failure is able to develop you and help you to explore the outer world. You are failing when you give up. As you make more mistake, you have learn more by trying again and becoming better with confidence then you will get what you dream for. When your family members or friends criticize you, you do not have to feel disappointed. You evaluate the critics, identify whether the critics are true. If it is true, accept and learn from it, and change it. If it is not, you can show them their mistakes of criticizing you.

Self-confidence is the inner self-management towards reality and positive of oneself and the world. People who are self-confidence have positive thinking, understand whom and how they are, trust in themselves, achievable goals, personality and strong will for development. We can maintain and build up our self-confidence by having favourable perceptions about ourselves and everything around us, conviction on your judgment and evaluation, hold on own self-concept, appropriate and real missions of life, and non-stop studying about life to increase standard of yourself. Self-confidence gives your power to live meaningfully. Self-confidence drives you to your dreams of successes. Although, self-confidence does not guarantee success, but, at least you have try to pursue what you wish for, and therefore, there is no regret at the end of your life. Therefore, close your eyes, think who you are and what do you want in your life, fill up your confidence and go after your dreams as time goes by fast and will not stop for you. On the other hand, you must know how to balance your confidence as do not have too much self-confidence, that is, overconfidence which may lead to failure too. It is improving and repairing your self-confidence, and not boost it up high.

REFERENCE :- Hawkins, J.M., Weston, J & Swannell, JC 1998, The Oxford Study Dictionary, Oxford University Press, Penerbit Fajar Bakti Sdn Bhd, Shah Alam.

2. <u>Turn towards reality</u> :-

1. Get the simple things right.

During training, Sunday was always depressing, because you knew the inevitable torture that Monday would bring. Monday was inspection day. To be successful as a SEAL, your attention to detail must be unwavering. So you start with the little things, like making your bed and cleaning the floors. I used to keep my bed impeccably made and sleep on top of the covers with a sleeping bag. If everything wasn't perfect, you paid for it. And sometimes when it was perfect, you paid anyway. The lesson: If you can't get the simple things right, you can't expect to successfully tackle more daunting tasks.

2. Set both realistic and unrealistic goals.

Successful people are relentless goal setters. They break down larger milestones into smaller, more achievable tasks. One of the most unrealistic goals a SEAL candidate can set is completing Hell Week. You don't sleep for a week. You run countless miles with boats, logs, and backpacks. You swim dozens of miles in the frigid ocean. You run the obstacle course daily and do more pushups and pull-ups than you can count. All while battling second-stage hypothermia, sores, and often fractures. Some students quit just minutes into Hell Week. You can't allow yourself to imagine what the end will look like. So you make–and achieve–one small goal at a time and pray for the sun to come up the next day. A series of near-term realistic goals will help you get closer to your big audacious ones.

3. Work hard.

This one seems obvious, but many people underestimate the level of effort it takes to be successful and achieve aggressive goals. It astonishes me that some of the guys showing up to SEAL training put no real time or effort into preparation. If you don't work hard preparing for potential success, you won't change that behavior when things get really tough.

A SEAL training class is broken down into boat crews of seven guys each: three on either side of the boat and a coxswain in the rear steering. During the first phase of training, you take the boats out through the surf and paddle miles up and down the beach every day. I was in a winter class, where the swells can be up to 10 feet or more. It takes every man digging in and paddling hard just to get through the surf zone without getting tossed upside down. When setting goals and pursuing success, you must sometimes lead and get others to paddle with you. You can't do it all alone. The minute you realize that you don't know everything and need help along the way, the better off you will be.

5. Don't make excuses.

Successful people don't make excuses for failure or shortcomings. They acknowledge their strengths and weaknesses and seek feedback from trusted advisers. The longer you sit around making excuses, the further you will drift from the possibility of achieving your goals.

6. Don't underestimate others.

One of the most fascinating things about SEAL training is that out of the couple hundred guys who start a training class, you could never hand pick the 30 or so who will graduate. Rarely is it the Rambo types who make it. Usually they are the first to go. Underestimating people, whether peers or competitors, is one of the worst things you can do. People who go far in life measure others by qualities such as integrity and strength of heart. Empower those around you, and you will be surprised by the outcome.

7. *Be willing to fail.*

When entering this phase of my life, I knew that statistically, the odds were not in my favor. I also knew that if I didn't try, I would never forgive myself. I decided that I would rather try and fail than be the guy who says, "I was thinking about trying that." You simply can't look at life through a lens of fear. If you take a calculated risk and fail, at the very least you have a valuable learning experience. Get back up. Dust off. And never, ever, be out of the fight.

SUCCESS:
A WAY OF LIFE

8. Embrace the repercussions of your actions.

On your path to success, you will make mistakes. One of my early mistakes was slacking off on my pushups after the obstacle course during the first day of the third phase of training. An instructor was looking through the rearview mirror while sitting in the truck. He was counting to see if I did the required 50. I decided to do 30-ish. That mistake earned me a spot with the "cheaters" the following week while at the shooting range. Each day, before we started, during lunch, and between drills, the cheaters would line up and sprint to the top of a nearby mountain in full gear. If you failed to make the cutoff time, you ran it again. It was torture. But the week after, I miraculously cut my four-mile run time by three minutes. Learn from your mistakes and turn the consequences into something positive.

3. _Self - love_ :-

1.

Talking to and about yourself with love.

2.

Prioritizing yourself.

3.

Giving yourself a break from self-judgement.

4.

Trusting yourself.

5.

Being true to yourself.

6.

Being nice to yourself.

7.

Setting healthy boundaries.

8.

Forgiving yourself when you aren't being true or nice to yourself.

4. <u>*Take your Time*</u> :-

1.

Express your needs. It's no one else's job to guess what you need.

2.

Question your guilt.

3.

Learn how to say no.

4.

Block out me-time each week (or every two weeks)

5.

Set boundaries at work.

6.

Implement an exercise routine.

7.

Make a date with yourself.

5. *Feel your feelings* :-

No one is exempt from experiencing emotions. That is a part of being here as a human. Why then, do so many people experience difficulty with feeling emotions fully? This might be because of a society that does not value feelings and prioritizes being "good" or "happy" above all else. Other factors can also affect our readiness to feel, like not being allowed to experience or show emotions growing up, or being told that feeling certain emotions like sadness, grief, or anger are "bad" and shouldn't be felt or expressed.

We eventually learn that emotions are the problem and when we do experience feeling things like sadness, embarrassment, or shame, we are also the problem. We learn to identify with them fully. We think "I am sad" as if we are that emotion. We think, "when I feel angry, I am an angry person. I don't want to be an angry person so I will not be angry." But we are not our emotions, even though we feel them. Repeat after me: We have emotions. We are not emotions.

What happens to emotions that have been suppressed? Maybe you've heard the saying, what you resist, persists. When we avoid or reject emotions, the energy of those emotions gets stuck in the body. This is why we continue certain cycles and unhealthy patterns. The energy is never released and stays with us until we fully allow ourselves to feel. What we resist, persists.

A common fear about allowing oneself to feel is that the feeling might last forever. All emotions will pass, we might feel one for a longer period of time (usually however long it was resisted), but it will always pass.

Whether you don't know how to feel your feelings, you don't want to feel your feelings, or you're struggling with feeling your feelings, we hope that this guide serves you in some way.

Validate yourself. - Feeling is a part of the human experience and all feelings are welcome to come and go. Acknowledge this, it might even help to repeat that to yourself. Validate what emotions are coming up for you by identifying it, welcoming it, and sitting with it, without judging it, without wanting it to change, and without thinking of a way to fix it. Remind yourself that it is safe to feel. One way to do this is by using "I" statements like "I feel ___ (insert emotion), it's okay that I feel (insert emotion), I am allowed to feel ___". Another way to validate emotions is to write the emotion you're experiencing in a letter. What would you say to guilt? What would you say to resistance? Speak to them kindly, validating their existence. Anything that is showing up is welcome.

Sit with your feeling.- Take 5 to 10 minutes to sit with your feeling. This feeling has been identified, validated, and now it's time to dig deeper. Ask yourself, "Where is this feeling in my body?" "Where am I holding tension?" "What does it look like?" "What color is it?" "How does this process feel?" If you find yourself thinking, "I just don't want to feel that." or "how do I even do this?" sit with that. That is how you're feeling. Go toward the thing that is blocking or frustrating you. Acknowledge it, validate it, and sit with it.

Express your emotions. - After you have identified your feeling, validated it, and explored where it is being stored, it's time to express and process. There are so many options for expressing and processing emotions, here are a few you can choose from. These activities might seem simple, but the real change comes in your intention. If you intend to use these to feel, you will.

6. _Ask for help_ :-

You're not alone, so you can find help. There's no need to feel ashamed for asking for help. Whether you choose to rely on a loved one, a stranger, a mentor, or a friend, there are people who want to help you succeed.

7. _Help others_ :-

Helping others is an important part of life; it gives you a sense of purpose and boosts your happiness while positively affecting the world around you. If you want to help others more but aren't sure where to start, look no further. Whether you're caring for friends and family or giving back to your community, keep reading for the complete guide to helping others.

.

Give friends and family help by offering comfort, listening, doing chores, and teaching them new skills.

.

Help your community by donating and fundraising for causes that you believe in. Volunteer your time as well.

.

Helping others allows you to connect with people and get a sense of purpose. The more you help people, the more accomplished you'll feel.

Ask people how you can help them:-

The easiest way to know how you can help others is simply to ask them. Talk to a family member or friend, ask them what they most need help with, and offer your services. Then, follow through and do whatever they've asked of you—actions speak louder than words!

.

Make a routine of asking around your circle of friends and family for what they need. Before long, helping others will simply be second nature to you!

Be proactive :-

Look for opportunities to help and lend a hand without being asked. Practice simple caring gestures, like calling your elderly grandpa to check in or bringing your friend dinner while they're sick. Don't wait for someone to ask for help—train yourself to think about all the different ways you can help people, so it becomes second nature. Focus on being as friendly as possible, and you'll get the hang of it!

Don't just look for ways to help the people you know. You could also hold the elevator door for a neighbor or offer to take a photo for a group of tourists if they're struggling with a selfie stick.

Teach skills to other people :-

Teaching others helps them learn valuable skills they might need in life. Offer to teach friends and family members who are struggling with a skill you know well, like helping your parents set up social media accounts or teaching a friend how to knit. Teach people outside your social circle, too—try tutoring a student in math, for example, or showing your coworker how to use the office copier.

.

Try not to sound condescending when you offer to teach someone—keep your tone casual and friendly, and say that you'd love to show them the ropes.

.

Get creative and use the internet to teach people too! For example, you could make a YouTube video about tie-dyeing shirts or post your special apple pie recipe on social media.

Comfort upset or grieving people :-

Comfort and compassion can make them feel better as they grieve. Be the first to offer condolences when someone you care about is suffering. Do what you can to give comfort, whether they need a hug, a shoulder to cry on, or a helping hand. Talk to them with empathy and compassion, and ask them if there's anything you can do to help.

For example, it might help a grieving friend if you bring them dinner a few nights each week or do something fun with them to get their mind off of the situation.

When you talk, say comforting things like, "I can't imagine what you're going through, but I want you to know that I'm here for you," or "I'm so sorry. Is there anything I can do to help you while you deal with this?"

Be a nonjudgmental listener :-

Sometimes, listening is more helpful and healing than practical assistance. Not everybody is looking for hands-on help or a solution to their problems; they just need to let out their feelings while a supportive friend listens. When someone is telling you about a hardship they're going through, listen actively and focus on understanding them rather than fixing their problems.

When someone is venting, they need a listener who won't judge them. Stay open-minded and think about how they must feel; judgment will make them feel like they can't trust you.

Don't interrupt or spend the time that they're talking thinking about your response. When you're a listener, giving the other person your full attention is important.

Do a chore for someone else :-

Tackling another person's chores is a great way to make their day easier. When people get busy or stressed, chores and jobs often slip through the cracks. Find out from your family and friends what they're too busy to do for themselves, and set aside some time to do the chore for them. Take care of chores without being asked, too—just look for a job that needs doing and take care of it.

This could be anything from cleaning up after dinner to mowing a lawn. You might surprise a family member and wash their car or make your spouse's lunch for them before work.

Say "thank you" and express appreciation

Receiving thanks makes people feel great about themselves. Plus, showing gratitude will make you happier too! Express your thanks when someone does something nice for you, and let your loved ones know how much you appreciate them even when there's nothing to thank them for specifically. Practice gratitude by creating a list of things you're grateful for and sharing them with others.

For example, send someone a quick "thank you" note if they give you a gift, or thank your friend for buying you dinner.

Make a social media post about how much you appreciate your spouse's support as you change careers, or tell a friend how proud you are that they ran a whole marathon.

Be especially nice to underappreciated people—like the person bagging your groceries or bussing your table at a restaurant. Their jobs are often thankless, but a few kind words might lift their spirits.

Volunteer for local organizations :-

Volunteer work improves your community as a whole. Look around for a charity you'd like to support, like a homeless shelter or soup kitchen, and spend time there doing whatever needs to be done. Not only will this help others, but it'll also give you a newfound appreciation for all the good things in your life—and it'll make you a more compassionate person.

Work at a battered women's shelter and help women and children who have had traumatizing experiences get back on their feet.

Try tutoring homeless children at the local shelter so that they can stay in school and not fall behind because the economy has been difficult for their families.

Volunteer for hospice and listen to the stories of the people who are going through their final days, or volunteer at a nursing

*home and ask to spend time with the
people who don't get visits from family.*

Donate to important causes :-

Donations let you help the community even if you can't volunteer. Pick a charity or organization that you'd like to support, and donate to it however you can. A donation doesn't have to be money (although you could certainly give money if you can afford to). Donate clothing to a local shelter, or bring non-perishable canned food to a food bank, for example.

.

Donate foods like unopened spices, canned soups, or beans.

.

Give toys to the local shelters and food banks. Many of the children who take refuge there don't have any toys of their own.

.

It's okay if you don't have money to spare! Don't strain yourself when there are other ways to help people. Instead, look through your unused items and set aside anything in decent condition that you can give away.

Redirect gifts and ask for charity donations instead :-

Use holidays and birthdays to raise money for important causes. It's always fun to get presents, but you could celebrate by helping others, alternatively. Ask your friends and family to make donations to charities rather than getting you gifts. Sure, you'll miss out on a few presents, but you can really make someone else's day instead!

You could even set up a fund that they can donate to. For instance, you might create a fund to help low-income children go to college.

7. <u>Make A Plan</u> :-

While you don't know what is going to happen in the future, you can always plan ahead. Look at the patterns in your life and see what challenges you've struggled with. Assess the optimal outcomes and make a plan for how you can achieve them.

If you work somewhere and can anticipate the types of challenges you may face, then you can plan ahead. This is the same for students in school. If a challenge is time management, then you can learn and plan for calendar management, for example.

8. <u>Work Smart, Not Hard</u> :-

Generally, there is more than one way to get something done. However, there's always just one optimal way or best way of doing it. To work smarter rather than harder, start by working backward. Outline and define your goal. Then, plan the process for how to get there. Perform research to see how others who have come before you have done it. Take count of your own skills and ideas for how you may be able to do it better. Then, stick to your path and get to work!

Why is Struggle important in our life ?

In today's world, there is a desire for comfort, and a fear of failure. People do not want to have to work at something again and again. Instead, they want to be able to do something right on the first try. If they cannot, often enough, they just quit. Although this avoidance of difficulty may seem harmless, it can have negative repercussions for future endeavors. Struggling with difficult problems leads to growth for future, seemingly unrelated, scenarios. Learning to struggle builds several skills

The first skill that struggling with difficult challenges builds is the ability to persevere through adverse circumstances. If students are taught to keep going even when they don't see an apparent way to solve a problem, they will grow in their ability to persevere. Although it may not benefit them immediately, this perseverance can be immensely useful later in life. For example, although struggling with problems in high school may not increase one's grade significantly or change one's circumstances, in college and in the workplace, the ability to keep plugging away at something can reap enormous benefits. In addition, as this skill develops, it continues to grow, giving greater and greater benefits.

BEST
SUCCESS
FAILURE

The second skill that struggling builds is adaptability. This is the ability to take multiple approaches to a problem, especially when the first attempt is not successful. When a student works on a problem, sometimes the first strategy fails, so the student must change tactics. This is akin to climbing a mountain. Sometimes, a path up the slope may look promising, but after following it a ways, it may turn out to be a dead end. Then, the climber must back up and try a different way. Eventually, he may find a way that works. However, if he had simply given up and left, he would not have been able to experience the excitement of reaching the peak. Clearly, the ability to adapt one's approach to a challenge can produce benefits. This sort of adaptability is key in solving many issues that arise in one's day-to-day life, as well as more major issues affecting the whole world.

Do you often wonder why we struggle and why struggling exists? I often wonder why we humans have to struggle to get what we want. I also think why is struggling a thing? Well, the struggle has always been a thing in my life and it is what made me what I am today. If it weren't for the struggles I faced, then I wouldn't be the person I am today. With struggles, I learned many new things and many new ways to get the things I want. The struggle is real in life and well it molds and shapes us humans from what actions we take and what decisions we make like it changes our whole lives like it did to me.

The struggle exists to change us and our lives and we struggle because it is the key to the path of our destination of what we want or what we want to become filled with challenges, knowledge, and so on. Without struggle, we humans won't be able to achieve what we have today. I believe that struggling in life is what keeps us humans alive and successful in life. I learned in school once that if you struggle; you learn and learning is the key to your success.

Struggling is unpleasant and uncomfortable, but there is no growth without it. When we "save" children from struggle, we prevent them from reaching their full potential. It's only through struggle that children learn to push past their comfort zone, develop persistence and problem-solving skills, and ultimately increase their capacity to reach goals and contribute to the world.

Without struggle, there is no gain, or transformation. Without struggle, our actions cannot coalesce, to harness the future. Without struggle, life is bland, and rudderless. Without struggle, we remain unprepared to meet the day's — or life's — challenges, and whatever magic we may have inside of us, it remains bottled up, untapped.

Struggle is central to our life force, and beauty. Without it, the world is a dull gray.

And yet: most of us are given to naturally avoiding struggle; or worse, spending our lives in an attempt to vanquish it, in search of peace, and ease.

There is nothing more empowering than struggle, met. In fact, knowing you have overcome something daunting, difficult, or horrific makes you psychologically and emotionally stronger. King; Gandhi; Yousafzai; McCain; Hawking; Fox... our history is full of true heroes who struggled to overcome prevailing limits, and advanced our collective humanity in the process.Every perceptual limit that we survive and surpass opens a new world of possibility to us. That's because most limits exist only in our minds.

We are too often our own biggest critics. We fear the unknown, and more often than not assume the worst — not the best — possible outcome. Regardless, once these imaginary obstacles are surmounted, the struggle we went through — whether that's our own mindset, or a form of physiological or intellectual learning — helps us to realize that we are better equipped to meet the world's challenges than we feared or knew. With that knowledge, our ability to aim our actions toward that which is most personally fulfilling to us improves.

Said another way, the more struggles we overcome, the closer we get to living the life we are meant to, because we find ourselves in the driver's seat of our own journey.

There is nothing — in my experience — that cements a friendship more than shared struggle. I have lasting relationships with people forged by no more than something powerfully difficult that we went through, together. Something funny happens when you emerge from a common trial. There is a significant intimacy that comes from this. The more difficult the trial, the deeper the bond — one that permeates all of your future interactions.

It's as though when someone sees us at our most vulnerable, the psychological urge to protect ourselves from one another suddenly vanishes. In a short period, your fellow 'traveler(s)' go from being "other" to "intimate".

Militaries capitalize on this. Soldiers who share a tour of duty often refer to themselves as "brothers" evermore, not because they necessarily share a background, but because of their shared experiences — their struggles. When something — money, opportunity, assistance — is given to us, the 'boost' that comes with it may be truly valuable, which itself is reason enough for gratitude. With that said, when we have done nothing to earn its presence in our lives, its value is limited. The Taoist proverb by Lao Tzu, "Give a man a fish and he'll eat for a day; teach a man to fish and he'll eat for a lifetime," comes to mind. When, on the other hand, our own actions have led to its procurement, additional dimensions of value emerge.

Not only do we learn from it and feel empowered. We further develop an appreciation for its costs (not only financial, but in effort), which serves to increase its value to us, including the sense of accomplishment. In my own life, I will always admire something I build — or help build — with my own hands, every time I see or use it, more than I will if someone else has done it for me, and I simply paid for it.

Whether it's a goal you set years ago, then worked hard to achieve, an emotional breakthrough that came from diligent self-care, a relationship that simply deepened after ages of nurturing it, or a physical artifact — a garden, a tool shed, a great meal, a painting, a manuscript — that you made with your own hands, these are the raw materials that lead to feelings of accomplishment.

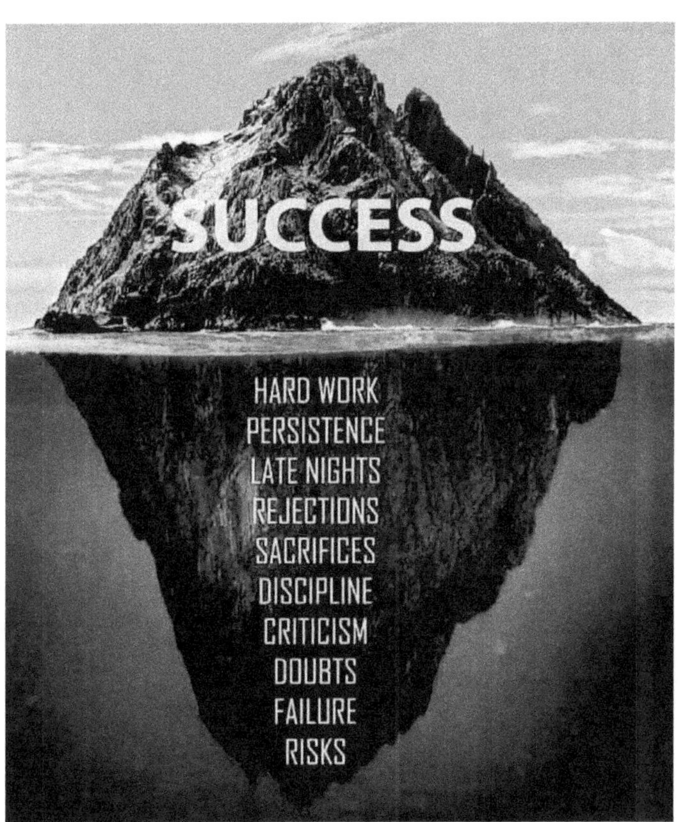

SUCCESS
HARD WORK
PERSISTENCE
LATE NIGHTS
REJECTIONS
SACRIFICES
DISCIPLINE
CRITICISM
DOUBTS
FAILURE
RISKS

It works for the recipient of such things, as well. Every parent (or friend or partner) prefers a hand-made or hand-written card, or gift, over one that's purchased. It's the effort if took to produce it that counts, because it makes us feel more valued. Many of us keep these things forever. Why? Something made by hand — not an assembly line — reaches deeper. Every effort, however modest, is a form of struggle over an easier alternative. And for its creator, the act becomes also more meaningful, as does the satisfaction of knowing we have the ability to manifest things of value for others. These are their own rewards.

Not every struggle has a Hollywood ending. Some overcome us. Others wipe us out, physically, financially or emotionally. And some struggles end up not being worth the cost to us, per se, whether or not we thought they would when we began our odysseys. This is great news. Not only does this teach us that not everything leads to success, or is worth our energy ("Pick your battles," as mom always says) but losing a battle delivers its own reward.

It humanizes us.

North Americans in particular are suckers for the conceit of the lone hero, overcoming impossible odds in just 90–120 minutes of film, or fewer minutes of television, to emerge from the fray, victorious. Europeans mostly roll their eyes at this concept.

Beyond movies — which are, after all, just representative of prevailing psyches and national narratives — failure is not only a great teacher from which we learn what not to do, as well as the value of our struggles; it is also, critically, a reminder that we are neither perfect nor omnipotent. That is, we are human; and a solid dose of humility is a wonderful thing.

When we demand success of ourselves, we are setting ourselves up for disempowerment. Demanding expectations is decidedly negative. When there's no room for anything but success, our (false!) feelings of self-worth are at risk. This is very different from choice. We can choose to do something because we want to. When we feel we must, it is no longer choice. Choices are open-ended, without preconceived results. Choices are healthy. Expectations seed self-hate. Dr. Theodore Rubin wrote a powerful book on this subject, titled Compassion and Self-Hate.

The only route to deep-seated wellbeing, ironically, is through utter self-acceptance, without stipulation. That applies to the parts we love about ourselves, and equally to those we don't. It's when we accept the parts that we don't yet love — this is self-compassion — that we can engage constructively with our acts.

In this context, struggles are choices borne of personal interest — the discovery of our inner landscapes, through outward exploration — instead of in response to some dictum or fairy tale idea of what it is to be human, or live a good life.

Struggles are their own reward. When we bump up against the limits of our capacity, we learn more about ourselves as an outcome of this process of self-discovery. This, in turn, builds capacity, regardless of direct results. We may think that the underlying reason we as a species continually seek or accept challenges is the specter of reward — of outcome. It's not so. We may think that busting our humps is all about securing our futures or those of our children — whatever economic or ethical form these take — but again, it's not so. Underlying all of this — the 'stated' cause for our efforts — is something deeper. We engage in living battles because it is only through effort and adversity — struggle — that our inner gardens flourish.

So to avoid struggle — to avoid giving in to the messiness, the unknown, the difficulties, the discomfort, the pain and the stress of it all — is to engage in the greatest act of self-subterfuge, or self-hate, of all. It is to rob us, in great measure, of the highest expression of our humanity: open-ended and full-tilt engagement with our world.

Struggles build perspective. Our trials allow us to act with increasing fidelity in our own lives. Feeding our inner gardens allows us to act, in turn, with power in the world. We don't have to be Thomas Edison and create 10,000 substandard light bulbs before illuminating the night.

We don't have to sit in meditation for decades before finally reaching samadhi, or enlightenment. We don't have to cure cancer, or put a man on the moon, or even win a battle, whether it's for "the fate of democracy", the right to vote, or control over the damned TV remote. These things are surely important. They may not be equally consequential, but even the remote, whose lessons include picking our battles, giving and relationships, has meaning.

But just as Sir Isaac Newton said, "If I can see a little further it is by standing on the shoulders of giants," it's not the outcome that matters, or the size of the trial, but rather the quality of our engagement with the world that matters. That's because as Newton intuited, we are all part of a continuity of human activity that started long before we were born and will continue long after we're gone. What we do to contribute while we are here is as important as the consequences attached to those acts are unknowable.

Poem's on Struggle

1. *Hard luck* :-

Ain't no use as I can see
In sittin' underneath a tree
An' growlin' that your luck is bad,
An' that your life is extry sad;
Your life ain't sadder than your neighbor's
Nor any harder are your labors;
It rains on him the same as you,
An' he has work he hates to do;
An' he gits tired an' he gits cross,
An' he has trouble with the boss;
You take his whole life, through an' through,
Why, he's no better off than you.

If whinin' brushed the clouds away
I wouldn't have a word to say;
If it made good friends out o' foes
I'd whine a bit, too, I suppose;
But when I look around an' see
A lot o' men resemblin' me,
An' see 'em sad, an' see 'em gay
With work to do most every day,
Some full o' fun, some bent with care,
Some havin' troubles hard to bear,
I reckon, as I count my woes,
They're 'bout what everybody knows.

The day I find a man who'll say
He's never known a rainy day,
Who'll raise his right hand up an' swear
In forty years he's had no care,
Has never had a single blow,
An' never known one touch o' woe,
Has never seen a loved one die,
Has never wept or heaved a sigh,
Has never had a plan go wrong,
But alas laughed his way along;
Then I'll sit down an'start to whine
That all the hard luck here is mine.

2. <u>**The Rainy Day**</u> *:-*

The day is cold, and dark, and dreary;
It rains, and the wind is never weary;
The vine still clings to the mouldering wall,
But at every gust the dead leaves fall.
And the day is dark and dreary.

My life is cold, and dark, and dreary;
It rains, and the wind is never weary;
My thoughts still cling to the mouldering
Past,
But the hopes of youth fall thick in the blast.
And the days are dark and dreary.

Be still, sad heart! and cease repining;
Behind the clouds is the sun still shining;
Thy fate is the common fate of all,
Into each life some rain must fall.
Some days must be dark and dreary.

3. <u>Don't Take It To Heart</u> :-

There's many a trouble
Would break like a bubble,
And into the waters of Lethe depart,
Did we not rehearse it,
And tenderly nurse it,
And give it a permanent place in our heart.

There's many a sorrow
Would vanish to-morrow,
Were we not unwilling to furnish the wings;
So, sadly intruding
And quickly brooding,
It hatches out all sorts of horrible things.

How welcome the seeming
Of looks that are beaming,
Whether one's wealthy or whether one's poor;
Eyes bright as a berry,
Cheeks red as a cherry,
The groan and the curse and the heart-ache
can cure.

Resolve to be merry,
All worry- to ferry
Across the famed waters that bid us forget;
And no longer tearful,
But happy and cheerful,
We feel life has much that's worth living for

yet.

SUCCESS

Success (the opposite of failure) is the status of having achieved. Success is the consequence of having earned a series of accomplishments.Being successful means the achievement of desired visions and planned goals. Life is nothing without success. Life has no taste if there ain't success. We can only achieve success if we fail one or two times. And this is true that failure can eventually lead to success, because we actually learn from our mistakes. uccess is "staying on course to your desired outcomes and experiences, creating wisdom, happiness, and unconditional self-worth along the way." Many people have different ideas of what success whether it is accomplishing a goal or having the perseverance to accept failure in the hopes of succeeding. Success can also be just being happy. While looking for your success it shouldn't be as easy as you thin.

In today's world everyone wants to be successful but what is a success. The perspective of success varies from person to person. For the record, the people before us have a different view on success and the person after us will have a different view on success.

Moreover, people compare different people performance to evaluate their success. But success is not something that you can copy from others. You have to make your own path to achieving success. In modern-day, people are obsessed with success because of the glamour and lifestyle of successful people.

There are many ways in the world to be successful. But most people think of celebrities, artist, politicians, and businessmen whenever they heard the word success.

Moreover, they think doing what they will make you successful but that not the case. They forget the most basic thing that makes a person successful that is their hard work, dedication, and the desire to achieve their dream. More importantly, they what they like to do not what that others told them to do. Successful people do what they like to do also they do what they feel correct for their business.

If you look in the dictionary for the meaning of the word success then you will find that it means the achievement of one's goal or aim. So, basically, anyone can achieve success by simply achieving their aim or goal.

Imagine if you got what you want, every time; no struggle, no hard work, and no challenges. No hard work required! some of us are saying that would be great. You would be weak and when something hard comes up in your life, you would not know how to handle it because you have never gone through anything that strengthens you.

So the point is, you can not grow without struggle. You can not develop strength without resistance, without challenging yourself, without struggle. Pain is your friend. May be not in the moment, but for the evolution of your soul, for the long term benefit of you, for a stronger human being, pain is your friend!

If you did not have failures, if you did not have struggles, if you did not have disappointments, you could have no strength, no courage, no compassion. Actually these qualities are made from your pain and struggle. You were given pain because you are strong enough to handle it. Life is given to you because you are strong enough to live it, because you are strong enough to drive through it, thrive through it and to inspire others through it. You have survived all of the challenges to this point and you will survive whatever is coming. But next time a struggle comes, I don't want you to curse the sky. Know that it was sent for a reason and a lesson. It might be to make you stronger, to teach you patience, it might be for you to show others your spirit. There is a reason! so don't you give up.

Success is nothing but the failure turned down and defeated. Success, in any ways, is the result of continuous struggles and patience on the side of a man who never gave up. Despite all this, it is also admitted that no success is ever lasting. One has to struggle and strive continuously to maintain success and be successful in career, relationship, study exams, life goals etc. The following Essay, I have written, on Success, its importance and what success means in career, relationship, life goals etc and how the students can be successful in life.

Success is a wholesome concept. It has a different meaning for everyone. It could be achieving your goals, getting what you want, or simply being happy and content with your life. But whatever it means to you, success is definitely worth pursuing. Success can be defined as the achievement of something you want or the realization of a goal. It could be a personal accomplishment, such as getting into your dream college or landing your dream job. Or it could be something larger, such as helping to improve your community or making a significant contribution to society. No matter what it is, success is definitely something worth striving for.

For a student, success stands for academic excellence with equal opportunities to shine in all fields of life. For an employee, success stands for getting the job done with perfection and moving up the corporate ladder. For a professional, success is all about making name and fame in chosen filed by acquiring required skills and acumen. But after academic achievement, the career pursuits become more important. The rat race to the top, or simply to make a good living, can be very demanding. Many people find themselves working long hours, sacrificing time with family and friends, and even putting their health at risk. It can be very tempting to give up and just accept what life has dealt you.

But success in career is not about working hard or sacrificing everything for your job. It's about finding a balance between your work and your personal life. It's about doing what you love and being rewarded for it. It's about making a difference in the world and feeling proud of your accomplishments.Ultimately, success in life comes down to being happy and content with your life. It's about finding a balance between work and play, between family and friends, and between your own needs and the needs of others. It's about doing what you love and feeling proud of your accomplishments. So don't be afraid to pursue your dreams, even if they seem out of reach.

Therefore, success is a multidisciplinary field. It evolves with your priorities change. It could be different for a student, an employee, or a professional. But one common goal unites all these groups, and that is to be content with what you have achieved in your life. And this could be anything from getting good grades to climbing up the corporate ladder. So don't give up on your dreams, and keep striving to achieve success.Being successful is something that everyone should aim for in life. Success doesn't just happen it takes a lot of hard work and determination to reach such an objective. You would need to master various skills that you need to know in order to be the expert at what you do, but that's only one side of the coin. Read the following Essay further, that describes what does it mean by being successful in life, meaning, purpose and what are necessary skills to be successful in Life.

Success comes in many forms. Some people want to become successful in their careers, while others have a passion for something else. Whatever your reason is, the goal is always the same... to be successful. And being successful takes hard work and determination. You must be willing to do what others are not willing to do. There are no shortcuts, so forget about the "get rich quick" schemes you see everywhere. You'll definitely get laughed at if you try to use them in real life. It may seem like an impossible task at first but once you set your mind to it and apply yourself, success will come knocking on your door.

Success will open many doors for you. It'll enable you to do the things that you want to do and to become who you want to be. Success is not measured by how big your house is or how fancy your car is; it's about happiness, fulfillment and satisfaction. You must also know that success is not permanent either, so make sure to enjoy it as much as you can before it's too late. Always remember that there is no such thing as "THE ONE". Success will come in many forms, and if you follow your passions and interests then success will find its way into your life. It may take some time but with hard work and determination anything is possible.

<u>*Success*</u>

*He has achieved success who has lived well,
laughed often and loved much:
who has enjoyed the trust of pure women,
the respect of intelligent men and the love of
little children;
who has filled the niche and accomplished his
task;
who has left the world better than he found
it;
whether by an improved poppy,
a perfect poem, or a rescued soul;
who has never lacked appreciation of Earth's
beauty
or failed to express it;
who has always looked for the best in others
and given the best he had.
Whose life was an inspiration;
Whose memory a benediction.*